MAO ZEDONG

First published in North America in 2007 by the
National Geographic Society
1145 17th Street N.W.
Washington, D.C. 20036-4688

Copyright © 2007 Marshall Editions
A Marshall Edition
Conceived, edited, and designed by Marshall Editions
The Old Brewery, 6 Blundell Street, London N7 9BH, U.K.
www.quarto.com

Trade ISBN: 978-1-4263-0062-2
Library ISBN: 978-1-4263-0063-9
Library of Congress Cataloging-in-Publication Data available on request.

Originated in Hong Kong by Modern Age
Printed and bound in Hong Kong by Midas Printing Limited

Publisher: Richard Green
Commissioning editor: Claudia Martin
Art direction: Ivo Marloh
Picture manager: Veneta Bullen
Production: Anna Pauletti

Consultant: Dr. Lars Laamann
Design and editorial: Tall Tree Ltd.

For the National Geographic Society:
Director of design and illustrations: Bea Jackson
Project editor: Virginia Ann Koeth

Previous page: Mao Zedong, 44 years old, pictured making a speech to Chinese troops fighting Japanese invaders in 1938.
Opposite: Members of the Red Guard reading Mao's *Little Red Book*.

MAO ZEDONG

THE REBEL WHO LED A REVOLUTION

FLORA GEYER

NATIONAL GEOGRAPHIC

WASHINGTON, D.C.

CONTENTS

BOY OF STONE

1

CHINA IN CHAOS

2

HUNGRY FOR POWER

3

PERMANENT REVOLUTION

在毛澤東的勝利旗幟下前進

4

BOY OF STONE

1

帶領一次革
命的反叛者

A Son at Last!

On the 19th day of the 11th month of the Chinese Year of the Snake, Wen Qimei whispered urgent prayers. She begged the kindly goddess Guanyin to let her new baby survive. This baby—a boy—was the third child she had borne, but the first two had both died.

Wen Qimei was a gentle, loving person, who mourned her two dead babies. Now she wanted a living child to cherish—and to do her duty as a wife. Like other Chinese women of her time, she believed she must produce a son. Her husband, Mao Yichang, expected it. A son would carry on the family name, make offerings to dead ancestors, and care for his parents when they became old or ill.

Wen Qimei's new baby was a healthy child, who showed no sign of dying. On the third day after he was born, she gave him his first bath.

Previous page: The farmhouse in Shaoshan where Mao Zedong was born.

Below: As a boy, Mao worked in terraced fields like these in Hunan. Peasant farmers cut the terraces into mountain slopes to stop heavy rainfall from washing the soil away.

1839–42 and 1856–60
China has confrontations with Britain, then Britain, France, and the United States, over trade and diplomacy issues.

1840 onward
European countries and the U.S. build concessions (trading settlements) in Chinese cities and ports.

Left: A proud father has his baby's horoscope read, in about 1900. The 12 signs of the Chinese zodiac are shown around the edges of the picture. Clockwise from top right, they are: Rat, Goat, Horse, Ox, Tiger, Snake, Boar, Monkey, Rooster, Dog, Rabbit, and Dragon.

After that, it was time to cast his horoscope, and give him a name. The horoscope recorded the pattern of the stars at the time of the baby's birth, and gave advice for his future. The choice of his name followed ancient Chinese tradition. The family name came first. It was Mao (which meant "Hair"), the same as most other families in the village of Shaoshan. The Mao clan had lived there for hundreds of years, mostly as peasants. The baby's personal name came next. It contained two syllables, or sounds: "Ze" meant "marsh," while "Dong" meant "the East."

Mao Zedong's birthday

Baby Mao's family recorded the date of his birth according to the Chinese calendar. This divides the years, which are named after 12 different animals, into 12 or 13 months, and counts time into cycles of 60 years. According to the Western calendar, Mao Zedong was born on December 26, 1893.

Wen Qimei hoped for a lifetime's good luck for her longed-for child. So she took him to a nearby rock, which villagers said was magical. She asked the rock to be her baby's second mother, and to protect him. From then on, she called her son "Shi San Yazi" (Boy Number Three, of Stone). All his life, Mao Zedong liked this name. It made him feel tough and strong.

1850–64
The Taiping Rebellion takes place, a lengthy civil war against the ruling Qing dynasty.

1863–77
Muslim tribes in western China rebel against the ruling Qing dynasty. Russia takes the opportunity to invade.

Tiger Valley

Baby Mao's home village, Shaoshan, lay hidden in a remote valley where tigers roamed free, in Hunan province, south China. Hunan was a beautiful place, with tall, misty mountains, slow, winding rivers, dense forests, and terraced fields.

At the time Mao was born, there were few main roads or railroads anywhere in China. It took Shaoshan villagers two days to travel 30 miles (48 km) to the nearest big town, on foot or by ox-cart. They needed weeks to reach China's capital city, Beijing, 1,300 miles (2,100 km) to the northeast. Hunan was just one of 20 Chinese provinces. Each had its own local customs, dialect, and accent. As Mao grew up, he learned to speak just like other Hunan peasants. He kept his rough Hunan accent for all of his life.

About 600 families lived in Shaoshan. Like Mao's father, they were nearly all farmers. As well as rice—their main crop—they also grew tea, bananas, and bamboo. Their homes were made of mud plaster and wood from local pine trees, with clay tiles on the roofs. Windows had no glass, but were covered with wooden shutters.

Left: Tigers, as seen in this 18th-century painting, were symbolic of strength and fierceness. In Hunan they lived deep in the forests, and rarely attacked people, but they did kill farm animals, such as sheep and goats.

1881–83
China invades Vietnam from the north. France invades from the south. They divide Vietnam between them.

December 26, 1893
Mao Zedong is born in the Hunan province of China.

Most homes in Hunan had no bathrooms, sinks, or clean water. Peasants dug holes in the ground for lavatories, fetched drinking water from streams or wells, and rarely bathed. They wore simple cotton clothes, wrap-over jackets with trousers for men or long skirts for women. The average peasant lifespan was just 35 years. Many babies died in the first weeks of life, including several of Mao's own brothers and sisters. Mao's parents had seven children: five boys and two girls. Both girl babies and the two oldest boys died; only Mao and two brothers, Zemin (born 1895) and Zetan (born 1905), survived.

Like other peasant boys and girls, Mao spent his first years following his mother around the house and into the fields. Once Mao could walk and run, he may have joined other children to go fishing, or to play with favorite Chinese toys, such as kites and soccer balls.

Clever and careful

Mao's family was not rich, but his father was clever and careful. He worked hard, spent little, and saved all he could. By the time baby Mao was born, his father had built one of the biggest houses in Shaoshan, and had set up a money-lending business, to add to his income from farming.

Below: A village street in China, photographed when Mao was a child and colored by hand later. Farmers are leading horses and donkeys laden with farm produce along an unpaved road.

1894–95
War between China and rival neighboring nation, Japan. China is defeated.

1894–95
Tonghak Rebellion, Korea. Korean rulers ask China to send troops to help them defeat rebels.

The Old Way of Life

Mao was born in a proud, ancient country. Chinese people called their land Zhongguo (the Middle Kingdom or Center of the World). They believed it was the most civilized place on Earth. For centuries, China produced brilliant scholars, artists, scientists, and inventors.

CONFUCIUS

The Chinese way of life had ancient origins. It was based on rules for behavior made by the philosopher Confucius (Kong Fuzi), shown here, who lived from 551 to 479 B.C. Confucius told Chinese people to work hard, fear the law, and honor their ancestors. That way, he said, good order would be preserved, and society would prosper. Confucius divided Chinese people into four separate groups. At the top, emperors, nobles, and scholars had a duty to rule well. In the second rank, peasants had to grow food for everyone. In the third rank, skilled workers made useful things to help others. Confucius put merchants at the bottom of society because they worked only to make money for themselves.

Above: The Great Wall of China was a symbol of China's wealth and power. It was first built in about 210 B.C. by the first emperor of the Qin dynasty (Shi Huang Di) to protect his lands from raids by hostile tribes. The wall was later rebuilt and extended to run for more than 4,200 miles (6,700 km).

Left: Peasant families kneel to show respect as a royal official is carried through their village in a splendid procession. In line with Confucius's ideas, scholars, government officials, and old people were honored. Wives had to obey their husbands. Children had to be polite and respectful. Chinese people believed that families were more valuable than individual men, women, or children. Everyone was expected to control their own feelings and actions for the good of other family members. Peasant sons did the same jobs as their fathers—and peasant girls were not valued like boys. Many were not even given a name. Mao's mother, for example, was just called Qimei, which means "Seventh Sister."

Right: Since 1420, China's emperors had lived inside the "Forbidden City," a high-walled cluster of palaces at the heart of China's capital, Beijing. Most emperors ignored Confucius's ideas and ruled badly. The scholars who worked for them as government officials were corrupt. As a result, millions of Chinese peasants led poor, miserable lives.

Farmer's Boy

In 1900, when Mao was six years old, he left Shaoshan and went with his mother to live with her family on their farm at Xiangxiang, about 16 miles (25 km) away. No one knows why Mao's mother left Shaoshan. Possibly, she missed her brothers and sisters. Perhaps she was unhappy living with Mao's father.

At his mother's family home, Mao learned many new skills. By now, he was old enough to make himself useful. So he helped his uncles as they worked on the farm. He fed the pigs with household scraps, and collected eggs from the ducks. He may also have gathered chillies, ginger, and garlic from the vegetable garden. Hunan food is famous for its strong, hot flavors.

In spring, young Mao paddled in flooded fields nearby, watching his uncles plant rice seedlings, which needed to be in water to survive. In the fall, he saw them harvest tall rice plants, and carry the grain back home. He walked beside their lumbering water buffalo as it pulled a heavy plow, and cut fresh grass to feed it. In his spare time, Mao learned to swim, and tried to catch fish in ponds and streams.

Buddhism

Buddhists follow the teachings of Buddha, a religious thinker who lived in India around 500 B.C. Buddha asked his followers to give up worldly things, be gentle, calm, and patient, and seek spiritual peace. Buddhist ideas arrived in China in about A.D. 100, and became very popular. As a child, Mao shared his mother's faith. But he gave up being a Buddhist when he reached his teens.

1898

The young Chinese emperor, Guangxu, starts the "Hundred Days" of government reform, but fails.

1899–1900

The Boxer Rising takes place. Chinese rebels attack foreigners throughout China.

Left: Chinese peasant farmers harvesting rice. They are pulling up the ripe rice plants, which have grown in specially flooded fields, and carrying them to their farmyards. There, the plants will be dried, then threshed (beaten to separate the rice grains from the stalks).

Indoors, Mao watched his mother and aunts cooking and cleaning. In the evenings, he sat with them as they spun cotton or mended torn clothing. While they chattered, Mao practiced making the shapes of Chinese characters, the symbols used for writing. His uncles were teaching him how to read and write.

On special occasions, Mao's mother took him to the nearby temple. She was a devout Buddhist. Together, they bowed to statues of Buddha and the goddess of mercy, Guanyin. They said prayers, burned incense, and set fire to paper money. The smoke carried their prayers to dead family members in heaven.

1900
Mao and his mother go to live with her family in Xiangxiang.

1901
The Boxer Protocol: Foreigners get compensation for the damage caused by the Boxer Rising.

Runaway Student

When Mao was eight years old, he and his mother went back home to Shaoshan. His father had decided it was time for him to start lessons. Mao's father was not well-educated—he had gone to school for only two years—but, like most Chinese people, he had a great respect for learning.

Mao's father wanted him to improve his mind, and perhaps train to be a scholar. He also wanted Mao to learn to keep accounts, to help the family business.

There was no public school in Shaoshan, so Mao's father paid for lessons with private teachers. This was expensive: only the richest peasants could afford it. Classes began in February, at the end of the Chinese New Year holiday. The pupils—boys, ages 7 to 17—sat together in a small room.

Right: Like other Chinese boys, Mao learned to add, subtract, divide, and multiply using a traditional wooden abacus. Each bead is an individual number; each wooden bar represents a group of 10. Calculations are made by moving the beads along the bars.

1902
Mao returns to Shaoshan and starts lessons with private teachers.

1904
Tibet demands independence from China. Britain supports Tibet's demands, favoring a weak China.

Their lessons were dull and very difficult. If they made mistakes or were fresh, the teachers beat them.

Mao and the other boys learned by memorizing lines from the Confucian classics. These were full of long words and complicated ideas, so they often did not understand them. However, they did learn to recognize and pronounce important Chinese characters. They also practiced handwriting, using a brush dipped in ink, and learned how to compose poems.

Bad behavior

Today, teachers and doctors might ask, "What made young Mao so angry?" or "Why did he run away from school?" But at the time Mao lived, people did not try to understand young boys' behavior. To them, Mao's rudeness and rebelliousness seemed simply wicked and shocking.

Mao liked studying. He was quick to learn and had a good memory. He loved history and old stories, and smuggled an oil lamp into his room, so he could read in bed. He also enjoyed writing (rather bad) poetry.

However, he hated the strict, unfriendly teachers. He was often rude and disobedient. Between the ages of 10 and 13, he ran away from school, or was expelled, at least three times.

Mao's mother begged her son to be good, while Mao's father was very angry. He said Mao was lazy, useless, ungrateful, and brought shame on the whole family. Mao paid no attention: He was sulky, defiant, and cold-hearted—characteristics that he would take to adulthood. He even threatened to kill himself, because he knew this would upset his father. It was clear from this early stage in his life that Mao was uncommonly talented, but had neither discipline nor respect for anyone.

1904–05
War between Russia and Japan. Japan defeats Russia and threatens northern China.

1905
The Western-educated Chinese doctor Sun Yat-sen sets up the Chinese Republican Party.

Getting Married

In 1907, Mao was expelled from school for arguing with his teachers. He was now nearly 14 years old, which made him an adult by the standards of the time. Mao's father decided that Mao must get married. Perhaps a wife would settle him down and make him less rebellious.

Mao's father also felt that it was time for Mao to start work. He told the boy that he must find a job and earn his own living, and suggested that he become an apprentice rice-trader. Mao hated the idea as he disliked hard physical work and thought country life was boring. So he made a deal with his father. He agreed to get married to any woman his father chose, if he could go on studying.

Mao's bride was a cousin, four years older than he was. She was known simply as "Woman Luo." Luo was her family name. Until they married, in 1908, Mao and Woman Luo had never met each other. She moved into Mao's father's home, but Mao refused to share his room with her.

Just over one year later, the unfortunate Woman Luo died. She was just 19 years old, and Mao was only 15. Mao did not mourn her death.

An ungrateful boy

Mao was 16 when he left his family to study in Xiangxiang, but he was not yet independent. His father paid for his education, food, and lodgings for the next 10 years—except for a few months, when, as a punishment, he stopped Mao's allowance. In spite of all their quarrels, Mao's father still thought it was his duty to help his son. Mao is not known to have thanked him.

1905
Sun Yat-sen, leader of the Chinese Republican Party, is exiled from China for his "dangerous" views.

1907
Mao is expelled from school.

Below: A Chinese wedding procession in about 1885. The bride is being carried in a curtained chair from her own family home to the house of her bridegroom's parents. Male members of her family walk alongside.

He was delighted to be single and free again. Mao asked his father to let him leave Shaoshan so that he could study at one of the new "modern" schools that were opening throughout China at this time. His father was persuaded that an education from a modern school would result in a well-paid job for his son.

These new schools taught subjects Chinese pupils had not studied before, such as Western science, sports, music, geography, world history, and foreign languages. In 1910, Mao went to a small modern school at Xiangxiang, close to his mother's family farm.

1908
Mao marries Woman Luo, who dies the following year.

1908
Empress Cixi dies. Army general Yuan Shikai rules China on behalf of child emperor Puyi.

CHINA IN
CHAOS

2

帶領一次革
命的反叛者

Amazing News

When Mao left home to study in Xiangxiang in 1910, he entered an exciting new world. Shaoshan was cut off from the rest of China by mountains and forests. The villagers had no newspapers and met few outsiders, and there were as yet no telephones or radios in China. But the teachers and pupils whom Mao now met came from many different places.

The other students were richer than Mao, wore up-to-date clothes—and had amazing news to share. Mao learned that Empress Cixi had died—two years earlier! Cixi had been a fierce, formidable woman. She had ruled China for her son, Tongzhi (died 1874), then for her nephew Guangxu (died 1908). Cixi had been a member of the Qing dynasty, which had ruled China since 1644. She had tried to isolate China from the rest of the world, and blocked attempts at government reform. As empress, she had had absolute power—and wanted to keep it that way.

Left: Qing Empress Cixi (1834–1908), portrayed when she was an old woman, around 1903. She boasted: "I have often thought that I am the most clever woman who ever lived... 400 million people depend on my decisions."

Previous page: This photograph shows Mao standing beside his father in 1910, when Mao was 16. He wears typical scholar's clothing: a long, loose robe over straight-legged pants.

1909
The U.S. tries to force China to allow American businesses to buy Chinese land and property.

1910
Mao goes to study in Xiangxiang.

Below: Chinese people who wanted government reform, including Mao and his student friends, cut off their traditional long pigtails, or braids, as a sign of protest against Qing rule.

Le Petit Journal

5 CENT. SUPPLÉMENT ILLUSTRÉ 5 CENT.

DIMANCHE 5 FÉVRIER 1911

LA CHINE SE MODERNISE
A Shanghaï, des chinois font en public le sacrifice de leur natte

Qing dynasty rule

Unlike most people in China, the Qing were not Han, or ethnic Chinese. Originally, they came from Manchuria, a country to the northeast. Most Qing ruled according to strict Confucian principles. They made all Chinese men wear long braided hair, called a queue. To cut of one's queue was a sign of rebellion.

At school, Mao read as much as he could about Chinese history. He learned about protests against Qing rulers, such as the Taiping rebellion (1850–64), in which 20 million people died, and about revolts by warlords. Mao also learned about the First Sino-British War (1839–42), between Britain and China, and the Arrow War (1856–60), with Britain, France, and the U.S. fighting China. These wars had blown up over arguments about trade and politics. Mao read how foreign interference in China angered many Chinese. They had set up a society, "Righteous and Harmonious Fists" (or "Boxers"), helped by Empress Cixi. In 1899, the Boxers had seized foreign property in China, but had been forced to surrender.

Now, in 1910, the new emperor, Puyi, was just four years old. New protests against the Qing, led by the Chinese Republicans, were growing stronger.

1910
Japan invades and conquers China's neighbor, Korea.

1911
Russians take control of Outer Mongolia, on China's northern frontier.

Revolution!

In 1911, Mao moved to a new school at Changsha, capital city of Hunan province. Here he heard thrilling news: there were plans for a revolution! The Republicans wanted to overthrow the new boy emperor and set up a reformed government, democratically elected by the Chinese people.

Mao was very excited. Like many other young students, he was impatient for change. He wanted to take part in politics and make things happen. He wanted to see the end of the old Qing dynasty and the traditional Chinese way of life. But he was not yet sure what he wanted the new, reformed, China to be like.

In October 1911, Republicans rioted in Wuhan, about 250 miles (400 km) northeast of Changsha. The riots soon turned into a full-scale revolution, as mobs seized Qing officials and attacked government buildings. With some student friends, Mao planned to travel to Wuhan. However, before they could leave, Republican soldiers peacefully took control of Changsha.

From 1911 to 1912, there was fighting around Changsha between Republicans and officials loyal to the Qing. In 1912, Mao joined a troop of Republican soldiers. His duties were running errands and fetching water.

The Revolution soon spread from Wuhan throughout China. In February 1912, the Republican leader Sun Yat-sen became China's first president, after Emperor Puyi agreed to abdicate. Just a few days later, Sun Yat-sen resigned as president, leaving the role to a tough old army commander, Yuan Shikai.

Mao left the army after six months. He wanted to be a student again. He went to several schools in Changsha, but left them all, without graduating.

1911
Mao goes to school in Changsha.

1911
Republican leader Sun Yat-sen returns to China from exile.

REVOLUTIONARY CHINA IN 1912

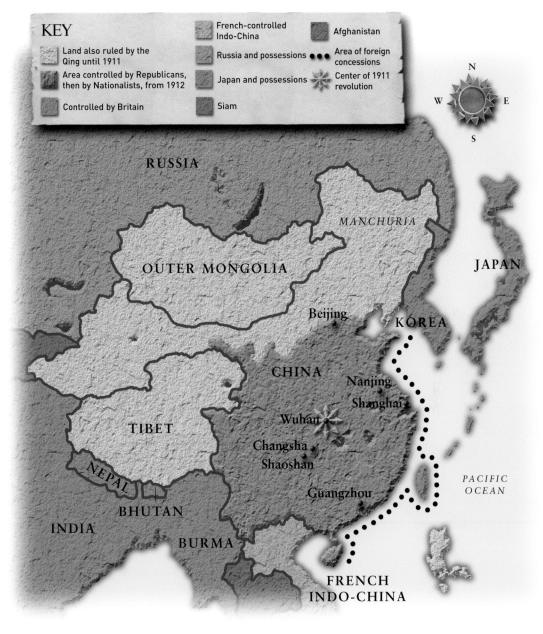

KEY

Land also ruled by the Qing until 1911

Area controlled by Republicans, then by Nationalists, from 1912

Controlled by Britain

French-controlled Indo-China

Russia and possessions

Japan and possessions

Siam

Afghanistan

• • • Area of foreign concessions

Center of 1911 revolution

RUSSIA

MANCHURIA

OUTER MONGOLIA

JAPAN

Beijing

KOREA

CHINA

Nanjing

Shanghai

Wuhan

TIBET

Changsha

Shaoshan

PACIFIC OCEAN

NEPAL

Guangzhou

BHUTAN

INDIA

BURMA

FRENCH INDO-CHINA

1911–12

The first Chinese revolution takes place.

1912

Mao joins the Republican Army for six months.

Political Crisis

For months after leaving the army in 1912, Mao had no job. He spent his time reading, writing, and talking with friends. He loved being free to do what he liked, but his father was furious and cut off Mao's allowance. To earn money, Mao decided to become a teacher, and enrolled at a teacher-training college in 1913. His father was relieved: At last it seemed as if Mao would have a proper profession.

Meanwhile, political upheavals continued to rock China. Song Jiaoren, one of Sun Yat-sen's associates, formed a new political party, the Guomindang

(Nationalists). Sun Yat-sen and many Republicans joined. In 1913, the Nationalists launched a second revolution, trying to overthrow Yuan Shikai. The Nationalists failed, and Sun Yat-sen and the other instigators fled to Japan.

Yuan Shikai ran the Chinese government until 1915, when he declared himself emperor. The Nationalists were horrified! The next year, Yuan died suddenly.

Left: Mao, at about 21, looking serious and determined. He had just qualified as a teacher, but had hopes of a career more dramatic than teaching.

1912
Sun Yat-sen is briefly president of China, before Yuan Shikai takes over.

1913
Mao starts to train as a teacher.

Right: The room at Beijing University where Mao worked as an assistant librarian in 1918 and 1919. His task was to sort and hand out newspapers and academic journals to leading scholars.

Rival army commanders, or warlords, fought for power. No one could control the whole nation, and soon China was in chaos. For ten years, there was war, as Nationalists, warlords, and a new Chinese Communist Party, which was founded in 1920, each fought to win power.

By 1915, Mao's mind was full of new ideas, both Chinese and foreign. He supported the Chinese Nationalists, joined student protest groups, and read books that called for new ways of life—without families, governments, or religions. He also became interested in the new, international political movement known as Communism.

In 1918, Mao moved to Beijing, where leading Communists lived. He found work in the university library there, and went to political meetings. He hoped to impress important people and become famous, but he failed, and returned to Changsha the next year, disappointed.

To survive, Mao worked as a primary school teacher, though he did not enjoy it. He also joined the teachers' trade union, which he found much more interesting. He edited the union newspaper and wrote articles for it. His favorite subjects included: "How should China be ruled?"

1914
World War I begins. Britain, France, and allies fight Germany and the Ottoman Empire (based in Turkey).

1916
Yuan Shikai dies. A period of chaotic warlord rule follows.

Communism

Communism is a political theory. It declares that people are born equal, and should have equal rights. It says that power and property should belong to the community, not to individuals, and that everyone should work as well as they can for the good of society. In return, they should be paid and cared for according to their needs.

Right: This Communist poster was painted in 1924 by a Russian artist. It shows working people from different lands advancing together toward a glorious future, protected by a huge red Communist flag.

KARL MARX

The great Communist thinker Karl Marx was born in Germany in 1818, but his revolutionary ideas made him very unpopular there. In 1849, he escaped to London, England, where he lived as a writer until his death in 1883. Communism was first discussed by thinkers in ancient Greece, but it only became popular after Marx published a short book called *The Communist Manifesto* in 1848. In this book, he described his own version of Communist ideas. Marx believed that history would progress, through economic and political upheavals, toward a perfect society run on Communist principles. Marx's work inspired many violent political struggles. The most important of these was the Russian Revolution of 1917, led by Vladimir Ilich Lenin (1870–1924), leader of Russia's Bolshevik party.

Right: In 1917, Russian people took part in a violent revolution. In this photo, troops loyal to the Russian tsar (emperor) fire on Communist protesters in the city of St. Petersburg. Communist fighters killed the tsar and his family, overthrew the government, and took control of all private property. This led to a civil war that lasted until 1921. In the years that followed, the Communist government completely reorganized Russian towns, villages, factories, and farms. Although this was intended to improve the lives of the majority, it led to much suffering, and millions of people died.

Left: Vladimir Ilich Lenin, head of the new Communist state in Russia, speaking to Russian soldiers and workers in 1920. In 1919, Lenin set up the Communist International movement, also known as the "Comintern." He aimed to spread Russian-style Communism all around the world. Comintern agents traveled to China in 1920, where they helped set up the Chinese Communist Party and recruit new members. Lenin invited Chinese people to Russia to train as Communist fighters. Communist ideas became fashionable among Chinese professors and students, including Mao. He joined the Chinese Communist Party in 1921.

Inside Mao's Mind

To most people he met, Mao Zedong seemed to be a really impressive young man. He had a clever brain, a quick wit, and a memory full of information. He was hard-working and ambitious. However, there was also a much more unpleasant side to Mao's personality.

Mao was very tall, with calm features and a strong, muscular figure. When he chose, he could work with great energy and determination. He liked outdoor sports, especially hiking and long-distance swimming.

Strangely, however, Mao usually dressed in torn, ragged clothes, and went unwashed, smelly, and dirty. He liked to swear and tell rude jokes. He did not seem to consider other people or worry about upsetting them—he was far more concerned with developing his political ideas.

Most shocking of all, in China at that time, Mao refused to do his family duty. From childhood, Mao had been rude and disobedient to his parents, and he did not become more considerate of them now that he was a young man.

Young Mao's writings also reveal a strange passion for violence and suffering. He longed for a "complete change" when everything—and everyone—would be destroyed to make way for a glorious new future. In 1921, when hundreds of people starved to death from famine in Changsha, Mao described their sufferings with cold-blooded fascination.

Mao did not believe he should have to live like other people. He did not want to work like them, or obey normal, everyday laws. "People like me only have a duty to ourselves," he wrote.

1918
Mao moves to Beijing, where he works in a library, before returning to Changsha the following year.

1918
A Communist government is set up in Moscow, Russia.

The only people Mao respected were dead heroes, such as the French Emperor Napoleon, who had conquered continents or started revolutions. He may even have dreamed of changing the world, like them.

Right: This image of Mao as a proud, stern young man, thinking deeply and far from the ordinary world, was painted when Mao was old and powerful. It shows how he remembered himself when young, and how he wanted others to see him.

A selfish son

In 1919, Mao's mother and father both fell ill and died soon after each other. Mao loved his mother, but did not visit her as she lay dying. He said he was too busy and that he did not want to remember her looking unwell. At her funeral, Mao told everyone that his father had been unkind to her. Mao never saw or spoke to his father again, although his family begged him to.

1920
The Chinese Communist Party is founded.

1920
Mao becomes headmaster of a primary school.

A Remarkable Wife

In 1920, at age 26, Mao was made headmaster of a small primary school. Later the same year, he married, for the second time. His bride, Yang Kaihui, had also been a student, but the family she came from was very different from Mao's. Her father was a respected scholar and had been one of Mao's professors at Changsha.

Above: Mao's second wife, Yang Kaihui (1901–30), with their two oldest sons, Anqing and Anying (standing). She wrote about Mao: "With his ability, his intelligence, he may even achieve immortal success... No matter how hard I try, I just can't stop loving him."

Yang Kaihui was a remarkable young woman: smart, pretty, thoughtful, loving, and brave. Many men wanted to marry her, but she chose Mao, probably because they shared an interest in revolutionary new ideas. Like Mao, Yang Kaihui was passionate about politics. Whereas Mao was very ambitious for himself, she simply hoped to make China a better place for all its people to live.

In 1922, Yang Kaihui had a baby— Mao's first son. Mao chose the name: Anying. It meant "outstanding person." They soon had two more sons, Anqing and Anlong. Yang Kaihui was devoted to Mao, but he had affairs with other women, and neglected her and their children.

1920

Mao marries his second wife, Yang Kaihui.

1921

Mao joins the Chinese Communist Party. He is also working for the Nationalists.

Politics was now keeping Mao very busy indeed. He was working as a local organizer for two rival revolutionary political parties: the Nationalists and the Communists. He was interested in both parties, because he thought that each might be useful to help him win power and change China.

Spying for the Russians

In 1923, the Communists sent Mao to work with the Nationalists in Shanghai. This was China's most exciting city, famous for its wealth. Now 29 years old, Mao had come a long way from his humble Shaoshan.

The Russian Communist government, who had pledged to support Communism around the world, paid Mao to recruit new Communists in China. This took up a great deal of time, so Mao gave up school-teaching in 1921. By 1922, he was head of the local Communist Party. The Russians also paid Mao to spy on groups of Nationalists.

Below: Tall, Western-style buildings line the busy road called the Bund in the city of Shanghai in the 1920s.

1921
Communists and Nationalists start to fight together against China's warlords.

1922
Mao becomes head of the Hunan Communist Party.

HUNGRY
FOR POWER

3

帶領一次革
命的反叛者

A Second Chance

It was New Year 1925, and Mao was miserable. He was back in his old home at Shaoshan, feeling bored, anxious, and ill. He had just lost his job working secretly for Russian Communists in China. They suspected that Mao did not believe, or understand, Karl Marx's original Communist ideas.

Mao spent eight months in Shaoshan, cut off from the rest of China, but his brothers kept him in touch with the latest political changes. In summer 1925, they brought news that a friend of Mao's, Wang Jingwei, had become one of the main contenders for leadership of the Nationalist Party. Mao and Wang had met while working for the Nationalists in Shanghai, and they had gotten along well.

Mao hurried to meet Wang and ask him for a job. He wanted a second chance to succeed in a political career. As Mao left Shaoshan, he was almost arrested and executed. The local governor accused him—wrongly—of leading riots against foreigners. Mao managed to escape alive.

From late 1925 to 1927, Mao worked for the Nationalists, who were fighting alongside the Communists against the warlords.

Previous page: Mao Zedong in 1925, when he was about to start a new job working for the Nationalists.

The White Terror

In April 1927, Nationalists attacked Communists in big Chinese cities. They thought the Communists were too powerful and were making trouble for Nationalist supporters in business and industry. Over 5,000 people were killed. These attacks became known as the "White Terror." White was the Nationalist Party's color; red was the Communists'.

1924

Chinese Communists and Nationalists make an agreement to join forces against the warlords.

1925

Nationalist leader Sun Yat-sen dies. Mao's friend Wang Jingwei is one of the contenders to take over as leader.

His task was to organize peasant protests in the south China countryside. As Mao traveled around, he witnessed many violent deaths, when peasants tortured and killed their enemies. He wrote that this violence gave him "a kind of ecstasy that he had never felt before."

At the same time, Mao also tried to win back favor from the Communists. He sent articles to newspapers, calling for a revolution to smash Chinese society. This pleased the Russians, and they helped Mao get an important job as a member of the Central Committee of the Chinese Communist Party.

Mao still liked working for the Nationalists. But in 1927, the Nationalist leader, Chiang Kai-shek, quarreled with the Communists and cut all ties with them. Angrily, he dismissed Mao and the rest of the Communists from the Nationalist Party, accusing them of being spies.

Left: A Chinese peasant family, dressed in padded cotton clothes, collapses from cold, hunger, and exhaustion. The Chinese Nationalists and Communists both hoped to recruit members from among poor, suffering people such as these.

1925
Mao is fired by the Russian Communists and returns to Shaoshan. He starts work for the Nationalists.

1927
The Nationalists dismiss Mao from his job.

Soldier and Politician

In 1927, Mao's life took a new direction. He became a soldier, working to spread Communism and advance his own career. Historians cannot agree which was more important to Mao. Some say Mao really believed that poor peasants would be helped by a simple kind of Communism. Others say he just used the Communist Party to win power for himself.

Below: Mao (far left) with the Communist army leader Zhu De (second from right) in 1930. Mao tricked Zhu's soldiers into following him, and plotted with Communist Russia to remove Zhu from his position as senior commander.

The Russians sent weapons and money to support the Chinese Communist Party, who began building up an army. Mao started to recruit his own soldiers. He knew that the more troops he had, the stronger he would be. Some of his men were peasants, who volunteered to join him, but Mao also hijacked troops from other Communist army leaders.

1927
Mao starts building up his own army.

1927
Mao abandons his second wife, Yang Kaihui. The following year he marries He Zizhen.

The Jiangxi Soviet

From Jinggang, Mao led his army west to Jiangxi. There, in 1930, he set up one of China's first "Soviets" (Communist states). All inhabitants had to belong to the Communist Party from the age of six. They were forced to attend mass meetings, to "educate" them in Communism.

Left: Mao gives a speech to peasant leaders in the Communist-controlled Jiangxi region in 1933.

There were millions of Nationalist Party members, but Chinese Communists only numbered a few thousand. After the White Terror, Communists were in danger from the Nationalists, and most went to live in remote places. Mao led his army toward the Jinggang Mountains of south China. In Jinggang, Mao lived comfortably in houses captured from rich local families, but his soldiers were cold and hungry. On Mao's orders, they treated mountain people cruelly. Homes and shops were destroyed and looted so that Mao could gather food and money. He also wanted to make everyone too scared to fight against him.

Other Chinese Communist leaders were furious with Mao for "stealing" their soldiers, but they were unable to stop him. In Russia, the Communists were delighted by Mao's rapid rise to power. Late in 1928, they declared that he should be leader of the Chinese Communist Army. Mao was now the best-known, and most feared, Communist in China.

1928
Nationalists set up a new government, based in the city of Nanjing, in eastern China.

1930
Mao sets up China's first Communist state, in Jiangxi.

Struggles for Power

Mao loved change, bloodshed, and suffering. They amused him, inspired him, and gave him energy. Mao was always fighting, scheming, or quarreling. He battled against anyone who got in his way.

Mao relied a great deal on Communist Russia for help. The Russian Comintern (international Communist organization) sent secret letters to guide him and money to pay his soldiers. Many Chinese Communists also backed Mao. Some thought that only Mao was strong enough to bring Communism to China. Some hoped to win Mao's favor and get a share of his power. Others supported Mao simply out of fear.

Mao distrusted all other ambitious men, including his Communist comrades. Although some of his comrades still admired him, many of them had grown to hate his cruelty and ruthlessness. Mao recruited his own secret

police to spy on his fellow Communists. He bullied them, together with their entire families.

Left: Mao (right) did have some loyal friends among the Communists. Here he was photographed with his trusted assistant, Zhou Enlai.

1930
Mao orders the killing of 3,000 Communist soldiers for supporting rival army commander Li Lisan.

1931
Mao's brother arranges for Mao's three sons to go to a Communist school in Russia after their mother is killed.

Right: Mao's enemy, Nationalist leader Chiang Kai-shek, photographed in 1928. That year, Chiang set up a Nationalist government, and claimed to rule all China.

However badly Mao treated them, they dared not disobey. He was known to have people who disagreed with him killed.

Mao also treated his own family with contempt and cruelty. In 1927, he abandoned his second wife, Yang Kaihui, soon after she gave birth to their third son. Three years later, she was arrested by the Nationalists. They offered to set her free if she spoke out against Mao. She refused, so they shot her dead.

Mao did not try to save Yang Kaihui or rescue his children. To him, they were all past history. In 1928, he had married again. His third wife was a teenage Communist student, named He Zizhen. Very soon, she realized that the marriage was a mistake. She tried to run away, but Mao sent soldiers to stop her.

Nationalist enemy

Among the Nationalists, Mao's chief enemy was General Chiang Kai-shek (1887–1975). From a wealthy merchant family, Chiang instructed the Republican army after the 1911 Chinese Revolution, and trained in Japan. From 1928, he led the new Nationalist government, which claimed to rule all China.

1931
The Jiangxi Soviet and other Communist republics are established, as forerunners of a Communist China.

1932
Japan sets up a new government in Manchuria, headed by the last Qing emperor, Puyi. He obeys the Japanese.

The Long March

Since 1930, the Nationalists had been trying to capture Mao's Communist state in Jiangxi. By 1934, they had surrounded it on three sides. Mao faced a difficult decision. Should he wait for the Nationalists to attack, then fight and probably die? Or should he lead his followers, including women and children, in a desperate bid for freedom? In October 1934, he ordered his Communists to leave Jiangxi.

Above: An iron-chain bridge over the Dadu River, in west-central China. Mao falsely claimed that his Communist troops had fought a victorious battle here.

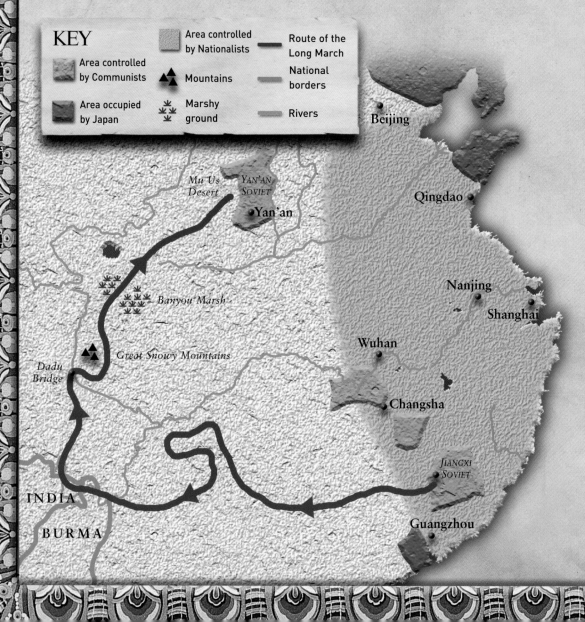

KEY

Area controlled by Communists

Area occupied by Japan

Area controlled by Nationalists

▲▲ Mountains

🌿 Marshy ground

Route of the Long March

National borders

Rivers

Mu Us Desert

YAN'AN SOVIET

Yan'an

Beijing

Qingdao

Nanjing

Shanghai

🌿 *Banyou Marsh*

▲▲ *Great Snowy Mountains*

Wuhan

Dadu Bridge

Changsha

JIANGXI SOVIET

INDIA

BURMA

Guangzhou

Right: This painting, made on Mao's orders when he was old and powerful, shows him making a speech to the troops on the Long March. The artist has added portraits of the Russian leader Lenin and the Communist thinker Marx on the wall, and a banner showing the Communist symbol, a hammer and sickle (farming knife).

Left: For most of the Long March, Mao was carried in a litter (portable bed), but his troops suffered horribly. Around 100,000 men and women set off from Jiangxi, but only 20,000 survived. The rest died from cold, sunstroke, hunger, exhaustion, accidents, or disease. Mao's third wife, He Zizhen, had to abandon their three children. She and Mao never saw them again. He Zizhen never recovered from the experience. In 1937, she left China for Russia, where she became mentally ill.

MARCHING FOR FREEDOM

The Communists walked for more than 6,000 miles (9,600 km). They crossed rivers, climbed mountain ranges, and struggled through treacherous deserts, bogs, and swamps. All the while, Nationalist soldiers followed them, ready to fight. Other Communist commanders joined the Long March, but Mao did not want them around. He sent his chief rival, Zhang Guotao, on a hopeless attack which ended in disaster. Zhang was disgraced, and 20,000 Communist soldiers died.

At last, after more than a year, the Long March ended at Yan'an, north China, in October 1935. The survivors of the march had no food, money, or land, and the Nationalist army was not far behind. Even so, the Long March was a personal victory for Mao. He used it to destroy rival Communist commanders and make himself Communist leader. Now, in 1935, he felt proud, independent, and strong.

The Japanese Invasion

In Yan'an, Mao ran another Communist state from 1936 to 1945. His Communist Party controlled everything, from food, clothes, and schools to transport and the army. Mao realized that the Party needed to find the respect and cooperation of all different classes, rich and poor: peasants, landowners, and business people.

Right: Mao's fourth wife, Jiang Qing (right), photographed in 1936 with her mother. The following year she met and married Mao Zedong.

Mao called life in Yan'an "glorious." Others described it as "a reign of terror." Mao kept hold of power by getting his followers to spy on their comrades, and denounce, or accuse, them for non-Communist thoughts or behavior. Mao also made people in Yan'an study his own writings. He wanted to teach them a new, Chinese type of Communism, independent from Russia.

In 1937, Mao married his fourth wife, Jiang Qing. She was a tough, glamorous actress with a scandalous past—and was not a loyal Communist. Mao's Communist comrades in Yan'an were horrified, but he did not care.

That same year, Japan invaded China. Rallying China's peasants to fight against the invaders, Mao's forces used guerrilla tactics behind Japanese lines.

1934–35
Mao leads 100,000 Communists on the Long March between Jiangxi and Yan'an.

October 1937
Mao's wife He Zizhen leaves for Russia. Mao marries his fourth wife, Jiang Qing.

Other Chinese Communist leaders also sent troops to join the battle, while the Nationalists agreed to fight alongside the Communists. Russia supported the Nationalists and Communists, as it too wanted to halt Japan's expansion. Russia was not happy with Mao as it distrusted his new "Chinese Communism," but they still backed him. In December, Japanese troops killed 30,000 people in the Nationalist capital, Nanjing.

Peasant power

In Yan'an, Mao thought about the best way to spread Communism. He realized that he must get Chinese peasants to support it. Peasants were the largest group in Chinese society. If they were organized by Communists, the party would have great power. Mao's Communist Party seemed to offer new hope, so many followed him.

After 1940, the Japanese also fought in World War II, against Britain and its allies. Beginning in 1941, these included the U.S. In 1945, the Japanese surrendered after the U.S. dropped atom bombs on the Japanese cities of Hiroshima and Nagasaki. The U.S. tried to make Mao's Communists and the Nationalists work together. But fighting between them continued from 1945 until 1949. Who would win, and rule over China?

Right: Invading Japanese troops with captive Chinese Nationalist soldiers and civilians, Shanghai, 1937.

September 1939	1945
World War II begins. Britain, France, and the Allies fight against Nazi Germany and Japan.	World War II ends. Germany, then Japan, are defeated, after the U.S. drops atom bombs on Japan.

PERMANENT REVOLUTION

4

帶領一次革
命的反叛者

在毛澤東的勝利旗幟下前進

The People's Republic

On October 4, 1949, Mao stood on top of the main gate of the Forbidden City, Beijing. For centuries, this splendid palace had been closely guarded. Only the emperor's family and their servants had been allowed to enter. Now Mao, the peasant farmer's son, was following in their footsteps. He was the new ruler of China. Far below, crowds chanted "Long Live Chairman Mao!"

How had this happened? It had been a bitter struggle. In 1945, after long years of fighting, the Nationalists and the Communists were both tired of war. But their leaders, Chiang Kai-shek and Mao, would not give in. The Communists controlled the countryside, but the Nationalists held most towns. Then, in 1948, Mao's troops captured the important cities of Shenyang and Xuzhou. The next year, they took China's capital, Beijing. The Nationalists were forced to surrender.

In his loud, gruff voice, Mao announced that China was now a People's Republic. Its 550 million citizens would be ruled by a Communist government.

Above: This photograph records the historic moment when Mao announced the formation of the People's Republic of China in October 1949.

Previous page: This poster, made in 1949, shows Mao smiling and waving, like a kindly father, to crowds of people cheering to welcome their new rulers.

1945

The Cold War begins: worldwide hostility between Communist nations and non-Communist states.

October 4, 1949

Mao proclaims the People's Republic of China in Beijing.

"When the enemy advances, we retreat. When the enemy escapes, we harass. When they retreat, we pursue. When they tire, we attack."
Mao on the battle for China between the Communists and Nationalists

In the years that followed, China's old ruling class—officials, landowners, and merchants—were driven from their jobs. Their property was handed to committees. The government ran all factories, shops, and farms, and controlled food, clothes, work, travel, education, and healthcare. Citizens had to back the Communists or risk losing their homes, jobs—and lives. Many peasants supported the new regime, hoping it would lead to prosperity for their families.

Mao wanted his new People's Republic to win respect. He also wanted to spread Communism all around the world. So, in 1950, he joined a new war, in Korea. He sent three million soldiers to help North Korea's Communists invade South Korea. At first they were successful, but the South was supported by United Nations troops. In 1953, the war ended, with Korea divided.

Below: Chinese Communist soldiers crossing a river in Korea, 1950. Out of the three million Chinese soldiers sent by Mao to Korea, around half a million died.

1949
Defeated Nationalist leader Chiang Kai-shek leaves China. He sets up a Nationalist government in Taiwan.

1950
Mao sends troops to help Communists in North Korea in their battle with South Korea.

The Great Leap Forward

Above: A starving peasant boy searches for rotting beans among muddy pebbles, during the famine caused by Mao's Great Leap Forward. The mass starvation of 1959-61 was the largest famine ever recorded.

Mao's Communist allies in Russia sent him weapons to fight in Korea. Mao also asked for Russian experts to help make aircraft and missiles and to develop new Chinese industries.

Mao said that he needed to modernize China's economy, which was still based on farming. There were few factories or machines. Secretly, he had another, more dangerous, aim. He wanted China to grow stronger than the Soviet Union—and to make nuclear weapons. With them, Mao dreamed, he could conquer the world!

In 1953, Mao's Communist government introduced a "Five Year Plan." This set targets for building new roads, bridges, dams, and factories. Peasants, who normally worked the land, were used to labor on vast construction sites.

In 1956 Mao asked China's best thinkers to suggest new ideas. "Let a hundred flowers bloom!" he said. But then Mao punished all who spoke out, and many thousands of clever people died. Was Mao frightened by new ideas, or by expert criticism? Or did he just plan to get rid of his enemies? No one knows.

1954–55
Nationalists in Vietnam, on China's southern frontier, are helped by Communists to defeat French rulers.

1955
Mao abolishes all peasant farms. They are joined together to become village "collectives," run by the government.

Either way, Mao refused to consult with any experts in the future. In 1958, he announced a new scheme called the "Great Leap Forward." It was to be run by Chinese peasants, and led by the Communist Party. That way, Mao could keep control. He also hoped to show that "Maoism" (his own, Chinese, version of Communism) could achieve great things.

The Great Leap Forward soon led to tragedy. Untrained peasants built bridges that fell down, machines that did not work, and badly made goods that no one wanted. The peasants had to abandon their farms in order to move into industry, so food production fell. At the same time, Mao sent food to other Communist states, to win friends and pretend that China was successful. After just two years, countless Chinese men, women, and children were starving; probably 38 million died.

Right: Peasants working with simple tools and bare hands to complete one of Mao's massive, useless, building projects. Around the same time (1959), Mao considered getting rid of peasants' personal names and giving them all numbers.

1958
Mao launches the Great Leap Forward.

1958
Mao groups collective farms into vast "communes." Each commune is run by a Communist committee.

Not Like Other Men

As ruler of the People's Republic, Mao was very conscious of the importance of maintaining a glorious personal image. His fame as the godlike "Chairman Mao," as he was now known, silenced his enemies and increased China's prestige. He also liked to be called the "Great Helmsman," who was steering Communist China to a golden future.

Mao had liked to think of himself as a special, superior person ever since his student days. The normal rules of good behavior had never applied to him! Ever since his early twenties, he had tried to force others to recognize his "greatness." That way, they would respect him, fear him, and obey his commands.

From the start of his career, Mao worked to create a good image. He wrote reports praising his own actions. Later, he invited writers from Europe and the U.S. to visit his Soviet states in Jiangxi and Yan'an.

Left: Mao (front of picture) swimming in the mighty Yangtze River in 1956. This was a carefully arranged publicity stunt to make Mao seem healthy and powerful. The official report, organized by Mao, described him looking like "an unshakeable mountain."

1959
The Communist Party tries to limit Mao's power.

1960
The Soviet Union cuts off technical aid to China.

Mao took great care to control what visitors saw: only the best farms, strongest soldiers, prettiest peasant women, and most charming children.

After Mao became ruler of the People's Republic, a glorious image was even more important. As before, Mao kept all information under close control. Beginning in the 1950s, newspapers, radio, movies, plays, and music in the People's Republic were all produced by Communists. They contained news or ideas that Mao wanted to be known, and words or pictures that praised him.

At the same time, Mao's own

Above: A false image, made of several separate photographs blended together, showing Mao surrounded by healthy, happy children. Some are wearing the red scarf of the Communist children's organization.

life was kept secret, even from his Communist comrades. He was seldom seen in public, except at Communist meetings or carefully staged "appearances." He spent most of his time in concrete, bomb-proof bunkers, surrounded by bodyguards. His rooms were filled with books as he loved reading. He often stayed awake through the night, and then slept until noon. No one was allowed to approach him, unless he gave permission—not even his fourth wife, Jiang Qing, or their only child, a daughter, Li Na.

1962
The Soviet Union builds missile bases on the Caribbean island of Cuba, nearly leading to war with the U.S.

1962
China invades India, on its southwest frontier.

The Cultural Revolution

In 1959, the Chinese Communist Party, horrified by the famine caused by the Great Leap Forward, tried to limit Mao's power. He was kept as official head of state, but was supposed to leave running the country to others. However, Mao was too strong, and kept hold of power. In 1960, Russia cut off technical aid to China, to show its disapproval of Mao. In 1962, a meeting of all the top Chinese Communists attacked Mao's policies. Mao was furious. In 1966, with the support of the Chinese army, he then launched a massive purge, or cleansing, of the Communist Party. He called it the Cultural Revolution. Mao invented a doctrine called "Permanent Revolution," which he said was aimed at getting rid of any supposed anti-Communists from among the Communist Party. In reality, he was taking revenge on the Communist Party for opposing him.

毛主席的革命文艺路线胜利万岁！

要使文艺很好
地成为整个革命机
器的一个组成部分，
作为团结人民、教
育人民、打击敌人、
消灭敌人的有力的
武器，帮助人民同
心同德地和敌人作
斗争

毛泽东

Left: A poster showing Red Guards attacking a supposed "enemy of the people."

RED GUARDS

The Red Guards were teenage students born or raised during Mao's time in power. They knew no other leader, and were blindly loyal to him. During the Cultural Revolution, Mao told the Red Guards to attack authority figures for poisoning their minds with "bourgeois" (anti-Communist) ideas. This was the first time that young people had been involved in Chinese politics, and they got very excited. No Red Guards dared to question Mao's violent orders, and so a terrifying mob rule got under way. From 1966 to 1969, Red Guards shamed, tortured, and murdered parents, teachers, doctors, writers, and Communist officials. They smashed schools, burned books, and wrecked works of art. They turned on fellow students, bullying or killing all who would not join them. Much of China's cultural heritage was destroyed, together with much modern knowledge. Millions of lives were lost or ruined.

Below: Red Guards pose for the camera after surrounding a group of peaceful Buddhist monks (in long robes, back of picture). Mao had been raised to respect Buddhist traditions, but during the Cultural Revolution he was eager to destroy all traces of China's past.

Above: Red Guards burning books which—they said—contained anti-Communist ideas. This rare Chinese news photo was taken in either 1966 or 1968.

Below: In October 1966, Mao approved army general Lin Biao's idea for a book containing Mao's sayings and writings. It became known as the *Little Red Book*, and was carried by all Red Guards. School children and peasants were made to learn its words and chant them out loud. It was displayed in all public buildings, from farm workshops to railroad stations. Anyone who did not honor it was treated as an enemy and risked exile or death.

The Leader Dies

By 1969, when the main onslaught of the Cultural Revolution was over, Mao was old and ill. He was nearly 76 years old, and years of indulgence had weakened him. He was a heavy smoker, abused sleeping pills, and ate rich meals. Now, he suffered from heart disease and an illness that slowly stopped him from walking and talking. But he would not give up power.

Mao did not trust anyone to run China in the way he wanted after he was gone. In 1969, he named general Lin Biao as his successor. But Lin plotted to remove Mao and rule China more moderately. Lin died in a mysterious plane crash over Mongolia in 1971.

After Lin's death, it seemed as if Mao's old friend and top diplomat Zhou Enlai would be the next leader. Unlike Mao, Zhou believed that China could learn from foreigners. He encouraged Mao to welcome overseas visitors, including U.S. President Nixon in 1972. But Mao grew suspicious of Zhou's plans. When Zhou fell ill, Mao would not let doctors treat him, so Zhou died, in January 1976.

Left: Old, frail, and ill, Mao greets U.S. President Gerald Ford on a visit to China in 1975.

1964–75
The Vietnam War: fighting between Communists (backed by China) and Nationalists (backed by the U.S.).

1964
China makes its own nuclear weapons.

The Leader Dies 57

The Gang of Four

The Cultural Revolution was led by Mao's fourth wife, Jiang Qing, who worked closely with three male colleagues, who together were known as the "Gang of Four." After Mao died, they plotted to seize power, but were arrested and put on trial. Jiang Qing killed herself in prison in 1991.

Below: Mao's wife Jiang Qing stands handcuffed to hear charges made against her in the Supreme People's Court, Beijing, in 1981.

Mao himself was cared for by specially chosen nurses. He feared that anyone else would try to poison him. However, just after midnight on September 9, 1976, Mao died. He was 82 years old. Since 1931, Mao had been the most powerful man in China; now he was gone. His body was put on public show, then mummified and displayed in a mausoleum dedicated to his memory.

To praise Mao's achievements, Chinese Communists arranged a splendid ceremony in Beijing. This was also designed to display China's strength and unity. But behind the scenes, the Chinese government was deeply divided. There were three rival factions. Mao's supporters wanted the Cultural Revolution to continue. Strict Communists wanted China to be run like Soviet Russia. Communist reformers, led by Deng Xiaoping, wanted Western-style policies to create wealth and encourage trade. The reformers won.

1966
The Cultural Revolution begins.

October 1966
Mao has his *Little Red Book* published.

Man or Monster?

Looking back at Mao's life, one top Chinese Communist said that Mao had been "seven parts right, three parts wrong." Mao did many terrible things and made many tragic mistakes, but his long career was also full of great achievements.

Mao helped end foreign control of China and remove an old, corrupt dynasty. He joined in building a new Communist Party, then led it toward victory. He united China after civil war, and restored Chinese pride. He won respect for China among foreign nations, and tried to modernize its economy. For the first

Above: A pro-democracy protester faces Communist government tanks in Tiananmen Square, Beijing, June 5, 1989.

time, he let Chinese peasants take part in politics, and gave rights to women.

However, to many people Mao was also a monster. He was extremely selfish and cruel. Most Chinese families had members who died so that Mao could win, or keep, power. Historians think that at least 70 million people perished because of Mao's policies. Mao's Great Leap Forward wrecked China's economy. His Cultural Revolution delayed China's development, destroyed millions of families, and did terrible damage to China's heritage.

Officially, Mao is still honored in China. However, today's Communist leaders have different aims. They want China to be powerful as an international trading nation, and, since the 1970s, the economy has grown astonishingly fast.

September 9, 1976
Mao Zedong dies.

1977
Communist leader Deng Xiaoping comes to power in China and begins Western-style economic reforms.

International Maoism

Rebels in many lands have copied Mao's idea of Permanent Revolution. In the 1960s, Maoist students in France led riots against the government. In the 1980s, Maoist "Shining Path" terrorists tried to take control in Peru. Today, Maoist rebels in Nepal are fighting to overthrow their king.

Today, China's economy is based on industry, not peasant farming. Chinese business people and foreign investors have built new roads, airports, and factories. Most Chinese people are better off than in 1949, when Mao came to power.

However, there are still many problems to solve. Industrial growth has led to pollution, corruption, and inequality. Most peasants are still very poor. City workers face cramped, unhealthy conditions in factories and dormitories, and daily dangers in building sites and mines. The media is still censored, religions are controlled, and political protesters are often punished. In spite of this, many Chinese people feel hopeful and positive. They are sure that their "Middle Kingdom" will have a great future.

Below: The Pudong business district in Shanghai. Until 1990, the whole Pudong area was farmland. Now it houses some of the tallest buildings in the world.

1978–80

The Chinese government sets up the first Special Economic Zone, in which private businesses can operate.

1985–91

New policies of *glasnost* and *perestroika* (openness and restructuring) transform the Soviet Union.

Glossary

abdicate resign, or give up ruling.

accent way of speaking.

accounts records of financial dealings, kept by businesses and some individuals.

ancestors family members who lived long ago.

apprentice trainee.

Bolshevik Member of the bolshevik ("majority") group within the Russian Communist Party.

bourgeois the middle class, seen by the Communists as greedy and oppressive.

boycott refuse to buy goods from, or refuse to speak to.

Buddhist followers of Buddha, a religious thinker who lived in India around 500 B.C.

characters writing symbols. Chinese characters are mostly ideograms—designs that represent an object or an idea.

collective farm several small farms joined together and run as one unit.

Comintern Communist international movement, set up after the Russian Revolution of 1917 to spread Communist ideas around the world.

committee a group of people chosen to carry out a particular task.

commune several villages in Mao's China that were joined together and run as a single unit.

Communist member of a political party in Russia (powerful from 1917) and in China (powerful from 1949). Communists wanted a government based on power for the people, with all property owned and controlled by the state.

concession land in 19th- and early 20th-century China controlled by foreign governments.

Cultural Revolution a mass movement, beginning in 1966, which was dominated by Mao's Red Guards. It was intended to revolutionize the attitudes of the people and destroy the power of China's authority figures. It involved terror, murder, and vandalism on a massive scale, encouraged by Mao and organized by his wife Jiang Qing and her allies.

democratic government a government chosen by, or ruling for, the whole people.

denounce accuse.

dialect words spoken only in one region of a country.

dynasty ruling family.

ecstasy thrill.

elected chosen by voting.

extremist a person who holds wild or extreme ideas.

Five Year Plan a feature of Communist-run economies. The government would set an ambitious plan for public works, industry, and agriculture. At the end of five years it was usually claimed that the plan had been a complete success to show the great achievements of the Communist system.

Great Leap Forward disastrous policy of industrializing China at breakneck speed starting in 1958.

guerrilla terrorist or other fighter who does not obey the normal rules of war.

homespun cloth made at home.

horoscope a prediction of future events based on observations of the planets.

manifesto book that sets out the ideas and policies of a political party.

Maoism a type of Communism invented by Mao Zedong. It gave power to the Chinese peasants, and called for a state of Permanent Revolution.

Marxism the teachings of German Communist thinker Karl Marx (1818–83).

mausoleum large building that houses the dead.

Nationalists a political party in China, powerful between 1928 and 1949.

peasants poor farmers. Most Chinese people were peasants in Mao's time.

Permanent Revolution one of Mao Zedong's policies. He called for Communists to continually criticize themselves and to spy on their comrades and families, in order to stop the spread of non-Communist ideas.

propaganda in Communist China, government-controlled information released to support Communist policies.

protectorate a region that is controlled by another, more powerful, country.

provinces regions of a country.

purged cleansed.

Red Guards mostly teenage student followers of Mao Zedong. They were excited by his ideas and encouraged to use violence to destroy China's institutions during the Cultural Revolution.

republican a system of government with an elected leadership.

revolution the overthrow of a government, usually by violence.

Soviet Communist-run state.

Soviet Union the USSR (Union of Soviet Socialist Republics). It included Russia and was the world's first Communist state. It lasted from 1922 to 1991 and, today, has split into many separate countries.

syllable single sound used to make words.

tsar emperor of Russia.

Bibliography

China: From Empire to People's Republic, Lynch, Michael, published by Hodder and Stoughton, 1996

The Chinese Revolution and Mao Zedong in World History, Malaspina, Ann, published by Enslow Publishing, 2004

Mao: A Life, Short, Philip, published by John Murray, 1999

Mao: The Unknown Story, Chang, Jung and Halliday, Jon, published by Jonathan Cape, 2005

Mao Zedong, Stewart, Whitney, published by Twenty-First Century Books, 2003

Mao Zedong (Judge for Yourself), Hatt, Christine, published by World Almanac Library, 2003

Mao's Road to Power: Revolutionary Writings 1912 to 1949, Schram, Stuart R. (ed.), published by M.E. Sharp, 1992

The Private Life of Mao Zedong: Memoirs of Mao's Personal Physician, Zhisui, Li, published by Chatto & Windus, 1994

Sources of quotes:

p. 30 Chang, Halliday, p. 13

p. 37 Chang, Halliday, p. 42

p. 49 Lynch, p. 55

Some Web sites that will help you to explore Mao Zedong's world:

www.kidskonnect.com/China/ChinaHome.html
www.pbs.org/wgbh/amex/china/peopleevents/pande03.html
www.time.com/time/time100/leaders/profile/mao3.html
www.chaos.umd.edu/history/toc.html
www.mrdowling.com/614china.html
www.royalty.nu/Asia/China/TzuHsi.html
www.friesian.com/confuci.htm

Index

Acknowledgments

B = bottom, C = center, T = top

Front cover: David King Collection

1 Getty Images/Hulton Archive; **3** Getty Images/AFP; **7** Topfoto/Roger Viollet; **8** Corbis/Keren Su; **9** The Bridgeman Art Library/Private Collection; **10** The Bridgeman Art Library/Bibilotheque Nationale, Paris; **11** akg-images/Waldemar Abegg; **12T** akg-images; **12B** Scala, Florence/HIP; **13T, 13B** Scala, Florence/HIP; **15** Scala, Florence/Free Library, Philadelphia; **16, 19** akg-images; **21** akg-images/Ullstein Bild; **22** Werner Forman Archive/Private Collection; **23** akg-images; **26, 27** David King Collection; **28T** Scala, Florence/Tretyakov State Gallery, Moscow; **28B** akg-images; **29T, 29B, 31, 32** David King Collection; **33** akg-images; **35** Rex Features; **37, 38** Getty Images/Hulton Archive; **39, 40** David King Collection; **41** akg-images/Ullstein Bild; **42T, 43T** David King Collection; **43C** Rex Features/Pacific Press Service; **44** Getty Images/Hulton Archive; **45** akg-images; **47** Art Archive/William Sewell; **48** Getty Images/AFP; **49** David King Collection; **50** Corbis/Arthur Rothstein; **51, 52, 53** David King Collection; **54** The Lordprice Collection; **55T** akg-images/Zhou Thong; **55C** David King Collection; **55B** Getty Images/AFP; **56** Getty Images/Hulton Archive; **57** Empics/Xinhua/Associated Press; **58** Corbis/Bettmann Archives; **59** Corbis/Xiaoyang Liu.